LETTING  GO

A Parents' Guide to Today's College Experience

LETTING

A Parents' Guide
to Today's College Experience

Karen Levin Coburn
and
Madge Lawrence Treeger

ADLER&ADLER

Published in the United States in
1988 by
Adler & Adler, Publishers, Inc.
4550 Montgomery Avenue
Bethesda, Maryland 20814

Library of Congress Cataloging-
in-Publication Data

Coburn, Karen Levin, 1941–
  Letting go.

  Bibliography: p.
  Includes index.
  1. College students—United
States—Psychology.
2. Parenting—United States. 3.
Parent and child—
United States. I. Treeger, Madge
Lawrence, 1934–
II. Title.
LA229.C53   1988   378'.198
87–19336
ISBN 0–917561–49–X

Printed in the United States of
America
First Edition

To our loving partners, Stephen and Tom . . . and Alison, Andrew, Anne, and Jennie, who continue to teach us about letting go.

CONTENTS

ACKNOWLEDGMENTS

We are deeply grateful to all the students, parents, and college faculty and administrators who have shared their insights and experiences with us. We have changed some of the identifying information to protect anonymity but you are the soul of this book.

In addition, we would like to thank the following friends and colleagues who have listened, questioned, critiqued, and continued to give their support during the last few years: Justin Carroll, Robert Easton, Rosemary Garagnani, Peggy Guest, Julie Jones, Meg Jacobs, Helen Kornblum, Ellen Krout-Levine, Marylen Mann, Marny Muir, Susan Rava, Linda Skrainka, Stephen Skrainka, Bob Sortland, Sally Stein.

We appreciate the active interest of our publishers, Esthy and Jim Adler, who had faith in us from the start. Our editor, Amy Pastan, with tact and care provided suggestions that helped the book take its final shape. And finally we give special thanks to our agent, Elizabeth Kaplan of Sterling Lord Literistics, who saw this project through from the kernel of an idea to its completion. She has been a constant source of good advice, enthusiasm, and encouragement.